Cataraqui United Church Cemetery 4

The Grave Whisperer

Angeline Gallant

Published by Angeline Gallant, 2022.

CATARAQUI UNITED CHURCH CEMETERY 4

First edition. October 23, 2022.

ISBN: 979-8215380246

Written by Angeline Gallant.

Also by Angeline Gallant

Calling Her Heart
Whisper of the Heart
No Turning Back
Forsake Me Not
Hear My Cry
Calling Her Heart Boxed Set Volumes 1-4

Keeper Of Secrets
A Lady's Secret

Midnight's Awakening
Heart of the Storm
Walking Through The Storm
Midnight's Awakening boxed set volumes 1-3

Secrets of the Underworld
Deklan's Dragons
Secrets of the Underworld Volumes 1 & 2

Tell My Story Collection
Tell My Story: England 1852

The Grave Whisperer
Wedding Bells in Kingston, Ontario, Canada 1923
St. Paul's Anglican Churchyard Kingston, Ontario, Canada A-B
St. Paul's Anglican Churchyard, Kingston, Ontario, Canada C - D
St. Paul's Anglican Churchyard, Kingston, Ontario, Canada G - H
St. Paul's Anglican Churchyard, Kingston, Ontario, Canada J - N
St. Paul's Anglican Churchyard, Kingston, Ontario, Canada O - R
St. Paul's Anglican Churchyard, Kingston, Ontario, Canada S - T
St. Paul's Anglican Churchyard, Kingston, Ontario T - Z
Small Graveyards & Burial Grounds: Kingston, Ontario, Canada
Cataraqui United Church Cemetery 1
Cataraqui United Church Cemetery 2
Cataraqui United Church Cemetary 3
Cataraqui United Church Cemetery 4

The Wolf Whisperer Series
The Cry of the Wolf
Captured Heart
Journey of the Heart
Fate's Legacy
Wolf Whisperer volumes 1 & 2
Endless White
The Wolf Whisperer Volumes 1-4

Standalone
Winds of Change vol 1-3

Table of Contents

MERCY (EVERETT) DALY[1]

Mercy was born in 1799.

She was 18 years old when her sister, Sarah Ann, passed away in 1817.

Mercy was 26 years old when her father passed away in 1825.

She was 38 years old when her mother passed away in 1837.

Mercy was 45 years old when her sister, Esther, passed away in 1844.

She was 47 years old when her husband passed away in 1846.

Mercy was 54 years old when her daughter, Charlotte Jane, passed away in 1853.

She was 55 years old when her sister, Mary, passed away in 1854.

Mercy was 60 years old when her brother, Charles, passed away in 1859.

She was 65 years old when her brother, John, passed away in 1864.

Mercy was 68 years old when Ontario was founded on July 1, 1867. Her son, George Wellington, passed away that same year.

She was 72 years old when British Columbia joined the confederation in 1871.

Mercy was 84 years old when she passed away in 1883.

STANLEY CHRISTOPHER DAVID[2]

S tanley was born in Kingston, Ontario on August 31, 1889.
He was 13 years old when he passed away on April 5, 1903.

CHARLES DAVID[3]

Charles was born in Kingston, Frontenac, Upper Canada, British Colonial America in August 1806.

He was 12 years old when his mother passed away in 1819.

Charles was 27 years old when he married Olive in Kingston on May 6, 1834.

He was 32 years old when he passed away in 1839.

DANIEL DAVID[4]

Daniel was born on August 14, 1790 in Fishkill, New York.

He was 28 years old when his mother passed away in 1819.

Daniel was 48 years old when his brother, Charles, passed away in 1839.

He was 62 years old when his sister, Nancy, passed away in 1853.

Daniel was 69 years old when his brother, Zachariah, passed away on April 27, 1860.

He was 77 years old when his sister, Belinda, passed away on June 17, 1868. His sister, Mary, passed away on September 19th.

Daniel was 80 years old when his brothers John and Samuel passed away in 1871.

He was 88 years old when he passed away in 1878.

ELIZABETH DAVID[5]

Elizabeth was born on March 29, 1791.

She was 75 years old when Ontario was founded on July 1, 1867.

Elizabeth was 79 years old when she passed away on July 8, 1870 in Lennox and Addington, Ontario. She is buried in Kingston, Ontario.

FRANCES NANCY "FANNY" (FAIRBANKS) DAVID[6]

Fanny was born on May 11, 1823. She was Dutch.

She was five years old when her brother, James, passed away in 1828.

Fanny was 14 years old when her brother, Christopher Isaac, passed away in 1837.

She was 22 years old when she married Zachariah David on October 20, 1847 in Kingston, Ontario.

Fanny was 32 years old when her sister, Jane, passed away in 1856.

She was 43 years old when Ontario was founded on July 1, 1867. Her father passed away on September 25th.

Fanny was 56 years old when her mother passed away in 1879.

She was 59 years old when the mining boom in northern Ontario began in 1883.

Fanny was 62 years old when her daughter, Matilda, passed away in 1886.

She was 65 years old when her brother, William James, passed away in 1888.

Fanny was 66 years old when her sister, Clarissa, passed away in 1889.

She was 72 years old when her brother, Caleb, passed away in 1896.

Fanny was 75 years old when her brother, Charles, passed away on February 4, 1899. Her husband passed away a few months later on November 22nd when she was 76 years old.

She was 76 years old when her daughter, Charlotte Mary, passed away in 1900.

In 1901 she was living in her son John's home in Frontenac, Ontario.

She was 78 years old when her sister, Lydia, passed away in 1902.

Fanny was 79 years old when she passed away in 1903. She was Methodist.

HENRIETTA (BULCH) DAVID[7]

Henrietta was born in 1863. She was Dutch.

She was three years old when Ontario was founded on July 1, 1867.

Henrietta was seven years old when her father passed away in 1870.

She was 19 years old when the mining boom in northern Ontario began in 1883.

Henrietta was 23 years old when she married John Wesley David on December 29, 1886.

She was 40 years old when her son, Stanley Christopher, passed away in 1903.

Henrietta was 42 years old when Ontario Hydro was established in 1906.

She was 52 years old when her sister, Sarah, passed away in 1916.

Henrietta was 56 years old when she passed away in 1919. She was Methodist.

JOHN WESLEY DAVID[8]

John was born in Kingston, Ontario in 1861. He was Dutch.

He was five years old when Ontario was founded on July 1, 1867.

John was 24 years old when his sister, Matilda, passed away in 1886.

He was 25 years old when he married Henrietta Bulch on December 29, 1886.

John was 38 years old when his father passed away in 1899.

He was 39 years old when his sister, Charlotte Mary, passed away in 1900.

John was 41 years old when his son, Stanley Christopher, passed away on April 5, 1903. His mother passed away a few days later on April 17th.

He was 44 years old when Ontario Hydro was established in 1906.

John was 48 years old when the Mann Act was passed in 1910.

He was 50 years old when his brother, William, passed away in 1912.

John was 58 years old when his wife passed away in 1919.

He was 68 years old when his sister, Emily, passed away in 1929.

John was 72 years old when the Dionne Quintuplets were born in 1934.

He was 74 years old when his siblings, Mary and Isaac, passed away in 1936.

John was 83 years old when he passed away in 1946. He was Methodist.

MABEL LOUISE (DAVID) BAUDER[9]

Mabel was born in Kingston, Ontario, on September 23, 1887. She was Dutch.

She was 15 years old when her brother, Stanley Christopher, passed away in 1903.

Mabel was 18 years old when Ontario Hydro was established in 1906.

She was 31 years old when her mother passed away in 1919.

Mabel was 32 years old when she married Ida Bauder on August 10, 1920 in Verona, Ontario.

She was 34 years old when her husband passed away in 1922.

Mabel was 58 years old when her father passed away in 1946.

She was 79 years old when her sister, Isabel Rose Elizabeth, passed away in 1966.

Mabel was 81 years old when she passed away in 1969. She was Methodist.

REBECCA (POWLEY) DAVID[10]

Rebecca was born in Kingston on December 20, 1795. She was 18 years old when she married Zachariah David in Kingston on May 3, 1814. Her father passed away on June 21st.

Rebecca was 42 years old when her brother, Rev. James Powley, passed away in 1838.

She was 50 years old when her sister, Hannah, passed away in 1846.

Rebecca was 53 years old when her sister, Elizabeth, passed away in 1848.

She was 62 years old when her brother, William Berrit, passed away in 1857.

Rebecca was 64 years old when her husband passed away in 1860.

She was 65 years old when her brother, Francis Thomas, passed away in 1861.

Rebecca was 69 years old when her sister, Mary, passed away in 1864.

She was 71 years old when Ontario was established on July 1, 1867.

Rebecca was 75 years old when her brother, Jacob, passed away in 1871.

She was 86 years old when she passed away in 1882.

ZACHARIAH DAVID[11]

Zachariah was born in New York on September 27, 1792. He was 21 years old when he married Rebecca Powley in Kingston, Ontario on May 3, 1814.

Zachariah was 26 years old when his mother passed away in 1819.

He was 45 years old when his father passed away in 1838. His brother, Isaac, passed away that same year.

Zachariah was 46 years old when his brother, Charles, passed away in 1839.

He was 60 years old when his sister, Nancy, passed away in 1853.

Zachariah was 67 years old when he passed away on April 27, 1860.

STANLEY CHRISTOPHER DAVID[12]

Stanley was born in Kingston on August 31, 1889. He was Dutch. He was 13 years old when he passed away on April 5, 1903. Stanley was Methodist.

ZACHARIAH DAVID[13]

Zachariah was born in 1825. He was Dutch.

He was 12 years old when his father passed away in 1838.

Zachariah was 20 years old when he married Fanny Fairbanks on November 3, 1845.

He was 20 years old when his mother passed away in 1846.

Zachariah was Methodist and a farmer.

He was 41 years old when Ontario was founded on July 1, 1867.

Zachariah was 60 years old when his daughter, Matilda, passed away in 1886.

He was 62 years old when his brother, John Jay Eli, passed away in 1888.

Zachariah was 74 years old when he passed away on November 22, 1899.

BARNABAS W. DAY[14]

Barnabas was born on January 27, 1816.

He was 23 years old when his sister, Catherine, passed away in 1839.

Barnabas was 26 years old when he married Susannah on February 23, 1842.

He was 29 years old when his sister, Harriett, passed away in 1845.

Barnabas was 32 years old when his sister, Roxanna, passed away in 1848.

He was 42 years old when his mother passed away on March 6, 1858. Barnabas passed away a few months later on October 29th.

BARNABUS DAY[15]

Barnabus was born in Goshen, New York on June 3, 1745.
He was two years old when his father passed away in 1748.
Barnabus was 17 years old when he married Polly Burdett in 1763.
He was 28 years old when his mother passed away in 1774.
Barnabus was 29 years old when his daughter, Mary, passed away in 1775.

He was a Loyalist.

GEORGE W. DAY[16]

George was born on November 14, 1930.

He was three years old when the Dionne Quintuplets were born in 1934.

George served as a staff sergeant.

He was 51 years old when the Canada Act was passed in 1982.

George was 75 years old when he passed away on July 21, 2006.

LEWIS DAY[17]

Lewis was born in Essex, New Jersey, on June 20, 1772.
He was two years old when his sister, Mary, passed away in 1775.

Lewis was 23 years old when he married Mary Polly Hill on September 8, 1795 in Kingston, Ontario.

He was 34 years old when his brother, Barnabas, passed away in 1807.

Lewis was 39 years old when the War of 1812 took place.

He was 77 years old when his mother passed away in 1850.

Lewis was 85 years old when his wife passed away in 1858.

He was 86 years old when he passed away in 1859.

MARY POLLY (HILL) DAY[18]

Mary was born on April 22, 1781.

She was 30 years old when the War of 1812 took place.

Mary was 51 years old when her brother, David Edward, passed away in 1833.

She was 57 years old when her daughter, Catharine, passed away in 1839.

Mary was 58 years old when her mother passed away in 1840.

She was 64 years old when her daughter, Harriett, passed away in 1845.

Mary was 67 years old when her daughter, Roxanna, passed away in 1848.

She was 76 years old when she passed away on March 6, 1858.

PERCILIA BLANCH (AYLESWORTH) DAY[19]

Percilia was born in Odessa, Ontario on April 8, 1882.

She was 23 years old when the FDA was created in 1906.

Percilia was 26 years old when she married William Henry in Kingston on September 26, 1906.

She was 29 years old when her mother passed away in 1911.

Percilia was 30 years old when the Central Banking System was established in 1913. Her daughter, Phyllis Irene, passed away on August 28th. Phyllis was only 18 days old.

She was 35 years old when her brother, David McKenzie, passed away in 1917.

Her brother, Charles Benjamin, passed away on March 1, 1918 when she was still 35 years old.

Percilia was 42 years old when her sister, Sarah Elizabeth, passed away in 1924.

She was 43 years old when her father passed away in 1926.

Percilia was 50 years old when her brother, Bowing Washington, passed away in 1932.

She was 51 years old when the Dionne Quintuplets were born in 1934.

Percilia was 68 years old when the ANZUS Treaty was signed in 1951.

She was 70 years old when she passed away on April 10, 1952. Percilia was Methodist.

WILLIAM HENRY DAY[20]

William was born in Kingston Mills, Kingston, Ontario on August 12, 1884.

He was 21 years old when Ontario Hydro was established in 1906.

William was 23 years old when he married Precilia on September 26, 1906 in Kingston.

He was 29 years old when his daughter, Phyllis, passed away in 1913. She was 18 days old.

William was 48 years old when his mother passed away in 1933.

He was 49 years old when the Dionne Quintuplets were born in 1934.

William was 67 years old when his wife passed away in 1952.

He was 70 years old when his daughter, Nellie Elizabeth, passed away in 1955.

William was 87 years old when he passed away on April 18, 1972.

PHYLIS IRENE DAY[21]

Phylis was born on August 10, 1913. She passed away 18 days later on August 28th.

POLLY (BURDETT) DAY[22]

Polly was born in Goshen, New York on June 3, 1745.

She was seven years old when her mother passed away in 1752.

Polly was 17 years old when she married Barnabus in Essex, New York in 1763.

She was 29 years old when her daughter, Mary, passed away in 1775.

Polly was 61 years old when her son, Barnabas, and brother, Oliver, passed away in 1807.

She was 80 years old when her brothers, John and Peter, passed away in 1826.

Polly was 104 years old when she passed away in January 1850.

EDNA PEARL (WARTMAN) DeLONG[23]

Edna was born in Kingston on February 23, 1899.

She was six years old when Ontario Hydro was established in 1906.

Edna was 16 years old when she married Richard in Kingston on October 11, 1915.

She was 17 years old when her brother, Harold, passed away in 1917. Her son, Harold, passed away on June 13th.

Edna was 18 years old when she passed away on October 18, 1918 in Belleville, Ontario. She is buried in Kingston.

HAROLD DeLONG[24]

Harold was born in Collins Bay, Ontario in 1916.

He passed away on June 13, 1917 in Kingston where he is buried. Harold was nine months and six days old according to his death record.

EDWARD BLAKE DENYES[25]

Edward was born in Ernestown, Ontario on March 18, 1887. He was German.

He was 18 years old when Ontario Hydro was established in 1906.

Edward was 32 years old when his father and sister, Brenda, passed away in 1920.

He was 35 years old when he passed away on September 11, 1922 in Ernestown. Edward is buried in Kingston. He was Methodist and a farmer.

HARVEY N. DENYES[26]

Harvey was born in Ernestown in 1844. He was Irish.

He was 23 years old when Ontario was founded on July 1, 1867.

Harvey was 32 years old when his sister, Ellen Amanda, passed away in 1876.

He was 34 years old when he married Mary Jane in Ernestown on February 3, 1878.

Harvey was 39 years old when the mining boom in northern Ontario began in 1883.

He was 43 years old when his father passed away in 1887.

Harvey was 45 years old when his mother passed away in 1889.

He was 62 years old when Ontario Hydro was established in 1906.

Harvey was 68 years old when his brother, Harvey Norman, passed away in 1912.

He was 73 years old when his brother, Sydney Albert, passed away in 1917.

Harvey was 74 years old when his sisters, Emily and Margaret Victoria and his brother John Wilson, passed away in 1918.

He was 75 years old when his brother, George, passed away in 1919.

Harvey was 76 years old when he passed away on May 8, 1920 in Ernestown, Ontario. He is buried in Kingston. He was Methodist and a farmer.

MARY JANE (JOHNSTON) DENYES[27]

Mary was born in 1851. She was Irish.

She was 15 years old when Ontario was founded on July 1, 1867.

Mary was 26 years old when she married Harvey in Ernestown, Ontario on February 3, 1878.

She was 31 years old when the mining boom in northern Ontario took place in 1883.

Mary was 51 years old when her father passed away in 1902.

She was 68 years old when her husband passed away in 1920.

Mary was 71 years old when her son, Edward Blake, passed away in 1922.

She was 73 years old when her mother passed away in 1924.

Mary was 75 years old when her son, Johnston Walter Day, passed away in 1926.

She was 80 years old when she passed away in 1931.

LEWIS DEWEY[28]

Lewis passed away on September 23, 1816.

SAMUEL DUTTON[29]

Samuel was born on May 23, 1853 in Lancashire, England.

He was 13 years old when Ontario was founded on July 1, 1867.

Samuel was 63 years old when he married Anna in Toronto, Ontario on September 4, 1916.

He is buried in Kingston, Ontario.

EDWARD NORMAN EASTMAN[30]

Edward was born in Winchester, Ontario on October 6, 1897. He was eight years old when Ontario Hydro was established in 1906.

Edward was 22 years old when he married Meda Vera Fern in Kingston, Ontario on September 21, 1920.

He was 36 years old when the Dionne Quintuplets were born in 1934.

Edward was 52 years old when his mother passed away in 1949.

He was 53 years old when his sister, Ethel, passed away in 1951.

Edward was 60 years old when his father passed away in 1958.

He was 70 years old when he passed away on September 20, 1967.

MEDA VERA FERN (AYLESWORTH) EASTMAN[31]

Meda was born on May 29, 1899. She was Dutch.

She was six years old when Ontario Hydro was established in 1906.

Meda was nine years old when her father passed away in 1909.

She was 20 years old when her brother, Norval Clarence, passed away in 1920.

Meda was 21 years old when she married Edward Norman in Kingston on September 21, 1920.

She was 34 years old when the Dionne Quintuplets were born in 1934.

Meda was 45 years old when her mother passed away in 1945.

She was 48 years old when her brother, Rupert, passed away in 1947.

Meda was 63 years old when her brother, Floyd John, passed away in 1962.

She was 68 years old when her husband passed away in 1967.

Meda was 73 years old when her brother, Wilbert Ross, passed away in 1973.

She was 79 years old when she passed away on July 24, 1978.

CALVIN HENRY EMMONS[32]

Calvin was born in 1878.

He was three years old when the mining boom in northern Ontario began in 1883.

Calvin was 19 years old when he married Margaret in Odessa, Ontario on November 16, 1898.

He was 27 years old when Ontario Hydro was established in 1906. His daughter, Eva Peal, passed away on March 4th. She was six years old.

Calvin was 28 years old when his daughter, Hazel Irene, passed away in 1907. She was five years old.

He was 43 years old when his brother, Francis Leonard, passed away in 1922.

Calvin was 47 years old when his sister, Florence Maud, passed away in 1926.

He was 50 years old when his brother, George Wesley, passed away in 1929.

Calvin was 51 years old when his mother passed away in 1930.

He was 55 years old when the Dionne Quintuplets were born in 1934.

Calvin was 63 years old when his brother, Charles William, passed away in 1942.

He was 76 years old when his brother, Edward Peter, passed away in 1955.

Calvin was 85 years old when he passed away on January 1, 1964.

MARGARET (GURNSEY) EMMONS[33]

Margaret was born in Rawdon, Ontario on March 24, 1878. She was German.

She was four years old when the mining boom in northern Ontario began in 1883.

Margaret was 10 years old when her father passed away in 1889.

She was 20 years old when she married Calvin Henry in Odessa, Ontario on November 16, 1898.

Margaret was 24 years old when her brother, Warren Allen, passed away in 1902.

She was 27 years old when Ontario Hydro was established in 1906. Her daughter, Eva Pearl, passed away on March 4th.

Margaret was 28 years old when her daughter, Hazel Irene, passed away in 1907.

She was 51 years old when her brother, Leamon, passed away in 1929.

Margaret was 55 years old when the Dionne Quintuplets were born in 1934.

She was 57 years old when her brother, Irwin, passed away in 1935.

Margaret was 62 years old when her sister, Nora Ella, passed away in 1940.

She was 68 years old when her brother, Harrison, passed away in 1947.

Margaret was 85 years old when her husband passed away on January 1, 1964. She was 86 years old when her sister, Harriett, passed away on July 16, 1964.

She was 90 years old when the Apollo moon landing took place in 1969.

Margaret was 91 years old when she passed away in 1970.

EDITH CATHERINE (DUFFY) EMMONS[34]

Edith was born in 1899.

She was seven years old when Ontario Hydro was established in 1906.

Edith was 13 years old when the Central Banking System was established in 1913.

She was 16 years old when she married William Byron on December 21, 1915 in Kingston.

Edith was 17 years old when her son, William Byron, passed away in 1917.

She was 33 years old when she passed away in 1932. Edith was Catholic.

WILLIAM J. BRYON EMMONS[35]

William was born in 1896.

He was seven years old when Ontario Hydro was established in 1906.

William was 19 years old when he married Edith Catherine on December 21, 1915 in Kingston.

He was 20 years old when his infant son, William Bryon, passed away in 1917.

William was 35 years old when his wife passed away in 1932.

He was 37 years old when the Dionne Quintuplets were born in 1934.

William was 52 years old when his father passed away in 1949.

He was 54 years old when the ANZUS Treaty was passed in 1951.

William was 56 years old when his mother passed away in 1953.

He was 87 years old when his sister, Lottie Pearl, passed away in 1983.

William was 88 years old when his sister, Mabel Elizabeth, passed away in 1985.

He was 90 years old when his brother, Ross Herman, passed away in 1987.

William was 92 years old when he passed away in 1989.

HERMAN ELLISON EMMONS[36]

Herman was born in Kingston in 1871.

He was 11 years old when the mining boom in northern Ontario began in 1883.

Herman was 19 years old when he married Bertha Victoria on September 22, 1890.

He was 34 years old when Ontario Hydro was established in 1906.

Herman was 79 years old when he passed away in 1951. He was Methodist.

BERTHA VICTORIA (RUTTAN) EMMONS[37]

Bertha was born in Loughborough, Ontario in February 1870. She was German.

She was 12 years old when the mining boom in northern Ontario began in 1883.

Bertha was 19 years old when the Woman's Suffrage movement began in 1890.

She was 20 years old when she married Herman Ellison on September 22, 1890.

Bertha was 35 years old when Ontario Hydro was established in 1906.

She was 36 years old when her brother, Arthur, passed away in 1906.

Bertha was 39 years old when the Mann Act was passed in 1910.

She was 49 years old when her father passed away in 1919.

Bertha was 50 years old when her sister, Rhoda Elizabeth, passed away in 1920.

She was 53 years old when her mother passed away in 1923.

Bertha was 54 years old when her brother, Charles Delbert, passed away in 1924.

She was 63 years old when the Dionne Quintuplets were born in 1934.

Bertha was 65 years old when her brother, William Burton, passed away in 1935.

She was 80 years old when her husband passed away in 1951.

Bertha was 86 years old when her sister, Mary Jane, passed away in 1957.

She was 95 years old when her sister, Ella Eurita, passed away in 1966.

Bertha was 96 years old when her brother, George Wellington, passed away in 1966.

She was 99 years old when she passed away in 1970. Bertha was Methodist and a farmer.

DOROTHY HELENA (ORSER) ERWIN[38]

Dorothy was born in Kingston on October 5, 1902.

She was three years old when Ontario Hydro was established in 1906.

Dorothy was five years old when the Bureau of Investigation was formed in 1908.

She was seven years old when the Mann Act was passed in 1910.

Dorothy was 31 years old when the Dionne Quintuplets were born in 1934.

She was 47 years old when her father passed away in 1950.

Dorothy was 60 years old when her mother passed away in 1963.

She was 85 years old when she passed away in 1998. Dorothy was Methodist.

MAJ. JOHN EVERETT U.E.[39]

John was born in Hamptonburgh, New York in 1744.

He was 35 years old when he married Mary Purdy in 1779.

He was a Loyalist and a major.

John was 41 years old when his father passed away in 1785.

He was 42 years old when the Shay's Rebellion took place in 1786.

John was 47 years old when the first parliament of Upper Canada assembled on September 17, 1791.

He was 61 years old when his mother passed away in 1805.

John was 73 years old when his daughter, Sarah Ann, passed away in 1817.

He was 76 years old when his sister, Esther, passed away in 1819.

John was 78 years old when his sister, Nancy Ann3, passed away in 1822.

He was 81 years old when the Crimes Act was passed in 1825. John passed away on June 28th.

MERCY (PURDY) EVERETT[40]

Mercy was born in New York on August 28, 1758.

She was 19 years old when her father, a Loyalist lieutenant, passed away in 1778.

Mercy was 20 years old when she married Major John Everett in 1779.

She was 32 years old when the first parliament of Upper Canada assembled on September 17, 1791.

Mercy was 54 years old when her mother passed away in 1812.

She was 58 years old when her daughter, Sarah Ann, passed away in 1817.

Mercy was 66 years old when her husband passed away in 1825.

She was 73 years old when her sister, Catherine, passed away in 1832.

Mercy was 78 years old when she passed away on January 11, 1837.

JOHN JAMES FERGUSON[41]

John was born in Inverary, Ontario on January 25, 1850.

He was 20 years old when British Columbia joined the confederation in 1871.

John was 70 years old when he passed away in Storrington, Ontario on February 4, 1920. He is buried in Kingston, Ontario.

MARTHA ANN FERGUSON[42]

Martha was born on February 1, 1850.

She was 20 years old when British Columbia joined the confederation in 1871.

Martha was 32 years old when the mining boom in northern Ontario began in 1883.

She was 55 years old when Ontario Hydro was established in 1906.

Martha was 70 years old when her husband, John James, passed away in 1920.

She was 83 years old when she passed away in 1934. Martha was Methodist.

MARY CATHERINE (HERCHMER) FITCH[43]

Mary was born on July 9, 1791.

She was four years old when her brother, Johan Jost, passed away in 1795.

Mary was 18 years old when her father passed away in 1809.

She was 20 years old when the War of 1812 took place.

Mary was 39 years old when she passed away on March 9, 1831.

NICHOLAS HERCHMER FITCH[44]

Nicholas was born on September 23, 1814.

He was nine years old when he passed away on December 6, 1823.

JAMES FLEMING[45]

James was born on Amherst Island, Ontario on August 8, 1839. He was Irish.

He was seven years old when his brother, Hugh, passed away in 1847.

James was 13 years old when his brother, William, passed away in 1853.

He was 27 years old when he married Mary Smith in Lennox and Addington, Ontario on December 4, 1866.

James was 31 years old when British Columbia joined the confederation in 1871. He was Methodist and a farmer living in Ernestown, Ontario at that time.

He was 34 years old when his daughter, Carrie Louisa, passed away in 1873. She was a year old.

James was 39 years old when his mother passed away in 1879.

He was 43 years old when his sister, Jane, passed away in 1882.

James was 49 years old when his brother, John, passed away in 1889.

He was 57 years old when his father passed away in 1897.

James was 66 years old when Ontario Hydro was established in 1906.

He was 77 years old when his wife passed away in 1917.

James was 89 years old when his brother passed away in 1928.

He was 90 years old when he passed away in Lennox and Addington, Ontario, on December 7, 1929. James is buried in Kingston.

MARY ELENOR (SMITH) FLEMING[46]

Mary was born on August 30, 1840. She was German/Irish/Dutch. She was 26 years old when she married James Fleming on December 4, 1866.

Mary was 31 years old when British Columbia joined the confederation in 1871.

She was 33 years old when her daughter, Carrie Louisa, passed away in 1873.

Mary was 42 years old when the mining boom in northern Ontario began in 1883.

She was 57 years old when her father passed away in 1897.

Mary was 76 years old when her brother, Tunis Hardy, passed away on March 16, 1917. She passed away a few months later on July 18, 1917 in Bath, Ontario. Mary is buried in Kingston. She was Methodist.

ETHEL DAY (RICKEY) FOLGER[47]

Ethel was born in Pittsburgh, Ontario on October 6, 1889. She was five years old when her brother, Archibald Augustus, passed away in 1895.

Ethel was 10 years old when her mother passed away in 1900.

She was 16 years old when Ontario Hydro was established in 1906.

Ethel was 31 years old when she married Collamer Creighton Folger on March 21, 1921. He was 46 years old.

She was 64 years old when her father passed away in 1954.

Ethel was 77 years old when she passed away in 1967. She was Methodist.

HANNAH (BELL) FRASER[48]

Hannah was born in Kingston, Ontario on October 20, 1830.

She was 22 years old when she married Thomas Fraser in Elizabethtown, Ontario in 1853.

Hannah was 36 years old when Ontario was founded on July 1, 1867.

She was 40 years old when British Columbia joined the confederation in 1871.

Hannah was 69 years old when she passed away in Toronto, Ontario on April 8, 1900. She is buried in Kingston, Ontario.

THOMAS GRANT FRASER[49]

Thomas was born in Kingston, Ontario in 1829. He was Scottish.

He was 38 years old when Ontario was founded on July 1, 1867.

Thomas was 42 years old when British Columbia joined the confederation in 1871.

He was Methodist and a farmer.

Thomas was 67 years old when he passed away in Toronto, Ontario on January 4, 1896. He is buried in Kingston, Ontario.

PERCY FREEMAN[50]

Percy was born in Ireland on May 17, 1899.

He was a year old when he passed away in Hinchinbrook, Ontario on July 21, 1900. He is buried in Kingston, Ontario. His father was a pastor.

ROBERT H. FRENCH[51]

Robert was born in 1917.

He was 17 years old when the Dionne Quintuplets were born in 1934.

Robert was 65 years old when the Canada Act was passed in 1982.

He was 78 years old when he passed away in 1995.

WILMA D. (GIBSON) FRENCH[52]

Wilma was born in 1925.

She was nine years old when the Dionne Quintuplets were born in 1934.

Wilma was 57 years old when the Canada Act was passed in 1982.

She was 70 years old when her husband, Robert, passed away in 1995.

Wilma was 82 years old when she passed away in 2007.

JOHN WILLIAM FRINK[53]

John was born in 1869. He was Dutch.

He was 13 years old when the Chinese Exclusion Act was passed in 1882.

John was 14 years old when the mining boom in northern Ontario began in 1883.

He was 28 years old when his sister, Isabella, passed away in 1897.

John was 33 years old when his infant son, Lorne Ernest, passed away in 1905.

He was 37 years old when Ontario Hydro was established in 1907. His infant son, Reginald Aubrey, passed away on July 12th. Reginald was two months old.

John was 39 years old when his father passed away in 1908.

He was 44 years old when the Central Banking System was established in 1913. His mother passed away on January 28th.

John was 63 years old when his sister, Olive, passed away in 1932.

He was 65 years old when the Dionne Quintuplets were born in 1934.

John was 75 years old when his brother, Robert Luke, passed away on April 14, 1944. His sister, Sylvia Adelia, passed away a few months later on June 13th.

He was 76 years old when his sister, Ethel Alberta, passed away in 1945.

John was 79 years old when his brother, James Richard, passed away in 1948.

He was 85 years old when his brother, David Henry, passed away in 1954.

John was 91 years old when his wife passed away in 1960.

He was 92 years old when his brother, Leonard Solomon, passed away on January 9, 1861. His sister, Eliza Jane, passed away on October 1st.

John was 94 years old when he passed away in Espanola, Ontario in 1964. He is buried in Kingston, Ontario. John was Methodist.

JULIA MAUDE (SMITH) FRINK[54]

Julia was born in January 1869. She was Dutch.

She was three years old when the mining boom in northern Ontario began in 1883.

Julia was 19 years old when she married John William on March 15, 1899 in Ernestown, Ontario.

She was 22 years old when her baby, Lorne Ernest, passed away in 1922.

Julia was 26 years old when Ontario Hydro was established in 1906. Her two-month-old son, Reginald Aubrey, passed away on July 12th.

She was 37 years old when her father passed away in 1917.

Julia was 39 years old when her mother passed away in 1919.

She was 54 years old when the Dionne Quintuplets were born in 1934.

Julia was 80 years old when she passed away in Espanola, Ontario in 1960. She is buried in Kingston, Ontario. Julia was Methodist.

BETTY (FULLER) JOHNSON[55]

Betty was born in 1920.

She was 14 years old when the Dionne Quintuplets were born in 1934.

Betty was 33 years old when Queen Elizabeth II was crowned in 1953.

She was 48 years old when her father passed away in 1968.

Betty was 58 years old when her mother passed away in 1978.

She was 62 years old when the Canada Act was passed in 1982.

Betty was 68 years old when her husband passed away in 1988.

She was 70 years old when she passed away in 1990.

[1] https://www.wikitree.com/genealogy/Everett-Family-Tree-6027

[2] https://www.wikitree.com/genealogy/David-Family-Tree-3143

[3] https://www.wikitree.com/genealogy/David-Family-Tree-4046

[4] https://www.wikitree.com/genealogy/David-Family-Tree-4047

[5] https://www.wikitree.com/genealogy/Unknown-Family-Tree-622234

[6] https://www.wikitree.com/genealogy/Fairbanks-Family-Tree-4322

[7] https://www.wikitree.com/genealogy/Bulch-Family-Tree-1

[8] https://www.wikitree.com/genealogy/David-Family-Tree-3173

[9] https://www.wikitree.com/genealogy/David-Family-Tree-3172

[10] https://www.wikitree.com/genealogy/Powley-Family-Tree-251

[11] https://www.wikitree.com/genealogy/David-Family-Tree-2742

[12] https://www.familysearch.org/tree/person/timeline/KD7K-M42

[13] https://www.wikitree.com/genealogy/David-Family-Tree-4008

[14] https://www.wikitree.com/genealogy/Day-Family-Tree-19472

[15] https://www.wikitree.com/genealogy/Day-Family-Tree-12053

[16] https://www.wikitree.com/genealogy/Day-Family-Tree-14137

[17] https://www.wikitree.com/genealogy/Day-Family-Tree-12054

[18] https://www.wikitree.com/genealogy/Hill-Family-Tree-52900

[19] https://www.wikitree.com/genealogy/Aylesworth-Family-Tree-384

[20] https://www.wikitree.com/genealogy/Day-Family-Tree-19374

[21] https://www.wikitree.com/genealogy/Day-Family-Tree-19476

[22] https://www.wikitree.com/genealogy/Burdett-Family-Tree-1311

[23] https://www.wikitree.com/genealogy/Wartman-Family-Tree-81

[24] https://www.wikitree.com/genealogy/DeLong-Family-Tree-3121

[25] https://www.wikitree.com/genealogy/Denyes-Family-Tree-34

[26] https://www.wikitree.com/genealogy/Denyes-Family-Tree-35

[27] https://www.wikitree.com/genealogy/Johnston-Family-Tree-26254

[28] https://www.wikitree.com/genealogy/Dewey-Family-Tree-3186

[29] https://www.wikitree.com/genealogy/Dutton-Family-Tree-4048

[30] https://www.wikitree.com/genealogy/Eastman-Family-Tree-918

[31] https://www.wikitree.com/genealogy/Aylesworth-Family-Tree-132

[32] https://www.wikitree.com/genealogy/Emmons-Family-Tree-2008

[33] https://www.wikitree.com/genealogy/Gurnsey-Family-Tree-116

[34] https://www.wikitree.com/genealogy/Duffey-Family-Tree-543

[35] https://www.wikitree.com/genealogy/Emmons-Family-Tree-2010

[36] https://www.wikitree.com/genealogy/Emmons-Family-Tree-1426

[37] https://www.wikitree.com/genealogy/Ruttan-Family-Tree-337

[38] https://www.wikitree.com/genealogy/Orser-Family-Tree-531

[39] https://www.wikitree.com/genealogy/Everett-Family-Tree-1850

[40] https://www.wikitree.com/genealogy/Purdy-Family-Tree-893

[41] https://www.wikitree.com/genealogy/Ferguson-Family-Tree-20318

[42] https://www.wikitree.com/genealogy/Unknown-Family-Tree-622564

[43] https://www.wikitree.com/genealogy/Herchmer-Family-Tree-15

[44] https://www.wikitree.com/genealogy/Fitch-Family-Tree-3967

[45] https://www.wikitree.com/genealogy/Flemming-Family-Tree-1146

[46] https://www.wikitree.com/genealogy/Smith-Family-Tree-288619

[47] https://www.wikitree.com/genealogy/Rickey-Family-Tree-356

[48] https://www.wikitree.com/genealogy/Bell-Family-Tree-38973

[49] https://www.wikitree.com/genealogy/Fraser-Family-Tree-12508

[50] https://www.wikitree.com/genealogy/Freeman-Family-Tree-3541

[51] https://www.wikitree.com/genealogy/French-Family-Tree-14875

[52] https://www.wikitree.com/genealogy/Gibson-Family-Tree-25971

[53] https://www.wikitree.com/genealogy/Frink-Family-Tree-737

[54] https://www.wikitree.com/genealogy/Smith-Family-Tree-288630

[55] https://www.wikitree.com/genealogy/Fuller-Family-Tree-18771

Don't miss out!

Visit the website below and you can sign up to receive emails whenever Angeline Gallant publishes a new book. There's no charge and no obligation.

https://books2read.com/r/B-A-QGSI-ULFCC

BOOKS 2 READ

Connecting independent readers to independent writers.

Also by Angeline Gallant

Calling Her Heart
Whisper of the Heart
No Turning Back
Forsake Me Not
Hear My Cry
Calling Her Heart Boxed Set Volumes 1-4

Keeper Of Secrets
A Lady's Secret

Midnight's Awakening
Heart of the Storm
Walking Through The Storm
Midnight's Awakening boxed set volumes 1-3

Secrets of the Underworld
Deklan's Dragons
Secrets of the Underworld Volumes 1 & 2